I Can Draw...
Sharks, Whales
&Dolphins

Artwork by Terry Longhurst

Text by Amanda O'Neill

This is a Parragon Publishing Book
First published in 2001

Parragon Publishing
Queen Street House
4 Queen Street
Bath BA1 1HE, UK

Designed, packaged, and produced by
Touchstone

Hardback: ISBN 0-75254-902-2
Paperback: ISBN 0-75255-613-4

Artwork by Terry Longhurst
Text by Amanda O'Neill
Edited by Philip de Ste. Croix

Printed in U.A.E

About this book

Everybody can enjoy drawing, but sometimes it's hard to know where to begin. The subject you want to draw can look very complicated. This book shows you how to start, by breaking down your subject into a series of simple shapes.

The tools you need are very simple. The basic requirements are paper and pencils. Very thin paper wears through if you have to rub out a line, so choose paper that is thick enough to work on. Pencils come with different leads, from very hard to very soft. Very hard pencils give a clean, thin line which is best for finishing drawings. Very soft ones give a thicker, darker line. You will probably find a medium pencil most useful.

If you want to color in your drawing, you have the choice of paints, colored inks, or felt-tip pens. Fine felt-tips are useful for drawing outlines, thick felt-tips are better for coloring in.

The most important tool you have is your own eyes. The mistake many people make is to draw what they think something looks like, instead of really looking at it carefully first. Half the secret of making your drawing look good is getting the proportions right. Study your subject before you start, and break it down in your mind into sections. Check how much bigger, or longer, or shorter, one part is than another. Notice where one part joins another, and at what angle. See where there are flowing curves, and where there are straight lines.

The step-by-step drawings in this book show you exactly how to do this. Each subject is broken down into easy stages, so you can build up your drawing one piece at a time. Look carefully at each shape before – and after – you draw it. If you find you have drawn it the wrong size or in the wrong place, correct it before you go on. Then the next shape will fit into place, and piece-by-piece you can build up a fantastic picture.

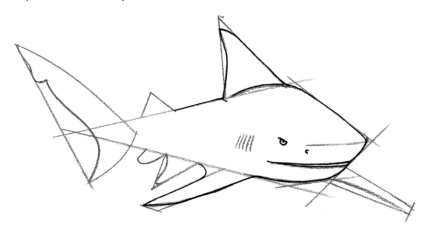

Tiger Shark

The Tiger Shark gets its name from its stripes. About twice the length of a real tiger, it is one of the biggest hunting sharks. It is also nicknamed the 'garbage-can' shark because it will eat absolutely anything.

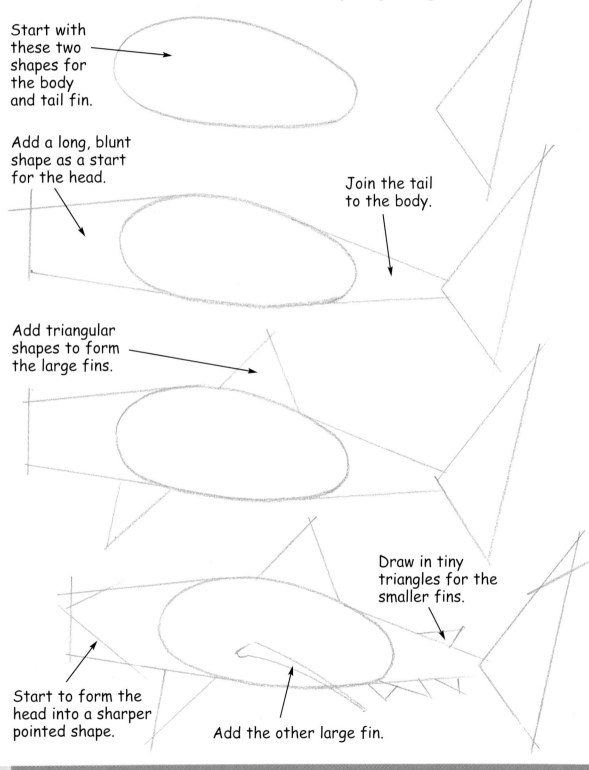

Start with these two shapes for the body and tail fin.

Add a long, blunt shape as a start for the head.

Join the tail to the body.

Add triangular shapes to form the large fins.

Draw in tiny triangles for the smaller fins.

Start to form the head into a sharper pointed shape.

Add the other large fin.

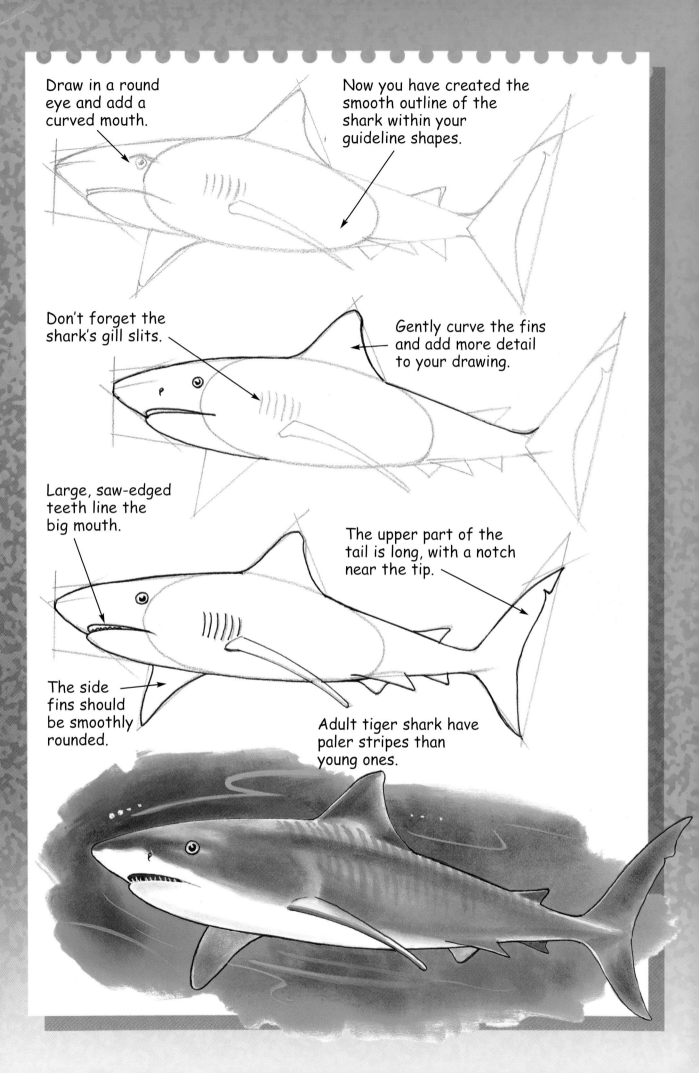

Draw in a round eye and add a curved mouth.

Now you have created the smooth outline of the shark within your guideline shapes.

Don't forget the shark's gill slits.

Gently curve the fins and add more detail to your drawing.

Large, saw-edged teeth line the big mouth.

The upper part of the tail is long, with a notch near the tip.

The side fins should be smoothly rounded.

Adult tiger shark have paler stripes than young ones.

Sperm Whale

This is the champion deep sea diver. It goes deeper than any other whale (at least 6500 feet) and can stay down for more than an hour before coming up for air. In the depths of the sea, squid are plentiful – and the Sperm Whale eats up to a ton of squid a day.

A diamond shape forms the huge head.

Now add a smaller triangle for the tail.

The head makes up about a third of the total length.

Join the whale's head to its body with two smoothly curving lines.

The flippers are small and paddle-shaped. Don't forget to draw in a small eye close to the flipper.

Start to smooth off the whale's outline and draw a large, flat mouth.

The tail divides into two sections called flukes.

The upper jaw is much longer than the lower.

Slightly roughen the outline along the back to suggest skin texture.

Teeth as long as a man's hand line the lower jaw.

The Sperm Whale is a slow swimmer, usually traveling at about our walking speed.

Your outline is now ready to color in.

Bull Shark

Many experts reckon this giant fish has attacked more people than any other kind of shark – perhaps because it feeds in shallow water, where more humans swim. It is the only shark that is just as happy in fresh water as in the sea.

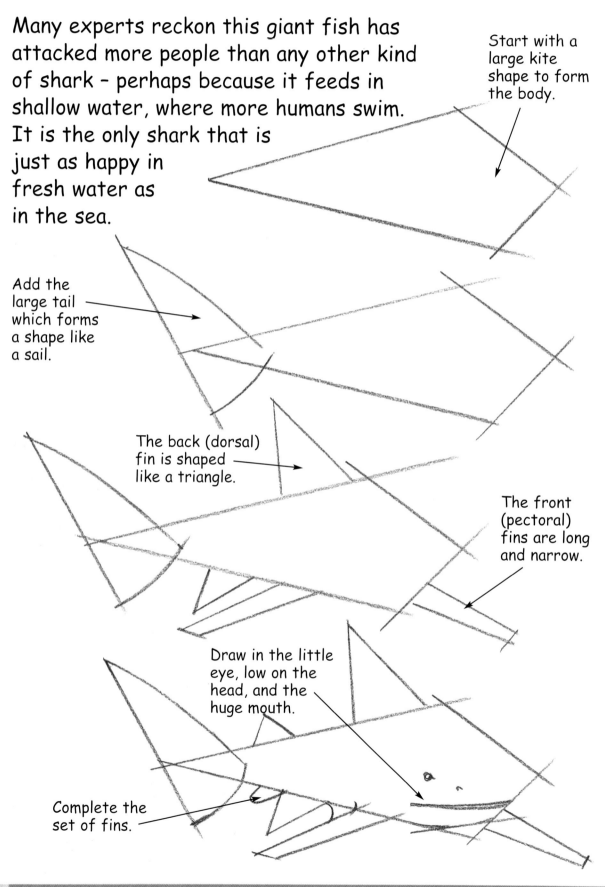

Start with a large kite shape to form the body.

Add the large tail which forms a shape like a sail.

The back (dorsal) fin is shaped like a triangle.

The front (pectoral) fins are long and narrow.

Draw in the little eye, low on the head, and the huge mouth.

Complete the set of fins.

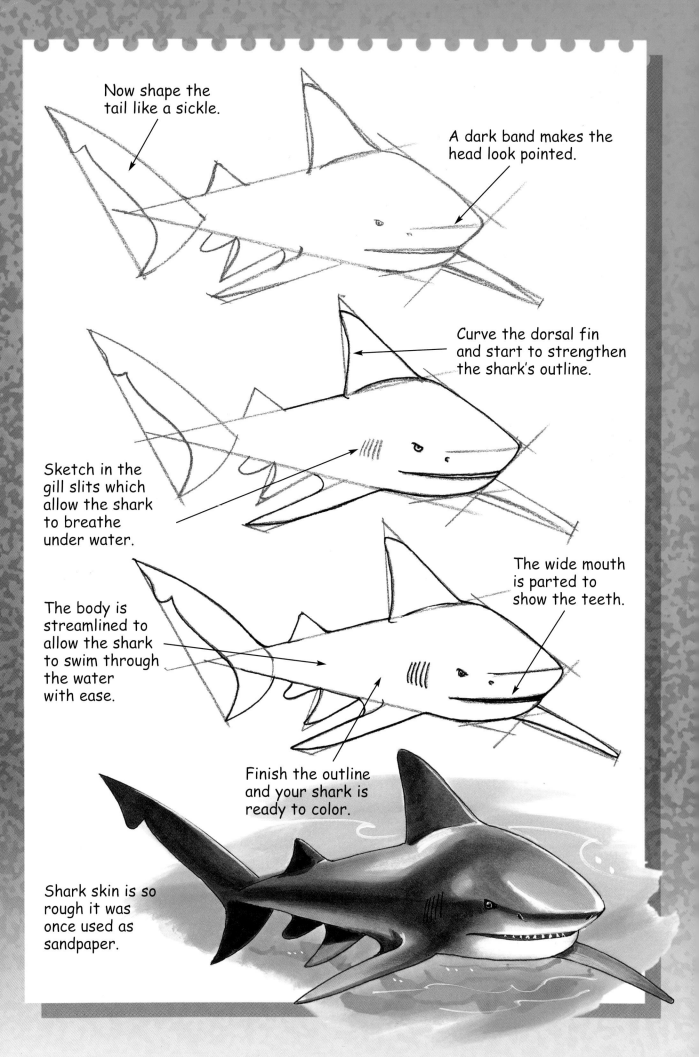

Now shape the tail like a sickle.

A dark band makes the head look pointed.

Curve the dorsal fin and start to strengthen the shark's outline.

Sketch in the gill slits which allow the shark to breathe under water.

The body is streamlined to allow the shark to swim through the water with ease.

The wide mouth is parted to show the teeth.

Finish the outline and your shark is ready to color.

Shark skin is so rough it was once used as sandpaper.

Dolphin

The dolphin is the acrobat of the ocean. Some species can leap as high as 20 feet (twice the height of an elephant) out of the water – and perform somersaults in mid-air.

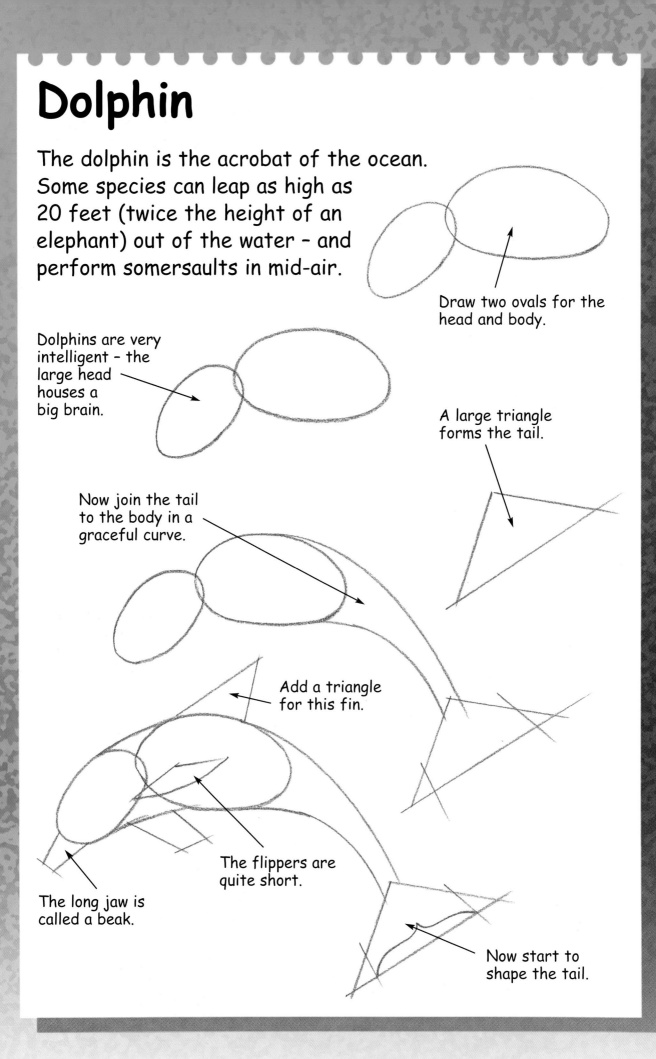

Draw two ovals for the head and body.

Dolphins are very intelligent – the large head houses a big brain.

A large triangle forms the tail.

Now join the tail to the body in a graceful curve.

Add a triangle for this fin.

The flippers are quite short.

The long jaw is called a beak.

Now start to shape the tail.

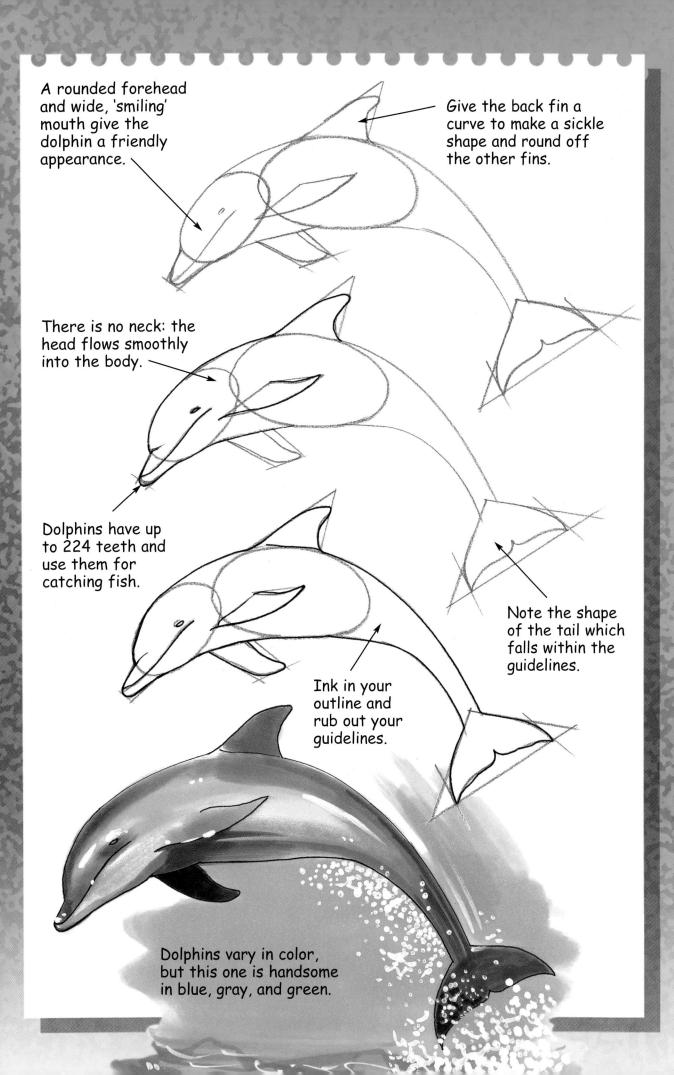

A rounded forehead and wide, 'smiling' mouth give the dolphin a friendly appearance.

Give the back fin a curve to make a sickle shape and round off the other fins.

There is no neck: the head flows smoothly into the body.

Dolphins have up to 224 teeth and use them for catching fish.

Ink in your outline and rub out your guidelines.

Note the shape of the tail which falls within the guidelines.

Dolphins vary in color, but this one is handsome in blue, gray, and green.

Gray Nurse Shark

The Gray Nurse Shark is a large hunter which takes all kinds of prey from fishes to other sharks. Like all sharks, it has a wonderful sense of smell. The tiniest trace of blood in the water will fetch it from a great distance, so it isn't a good idea to bleed in shark-infested waters!

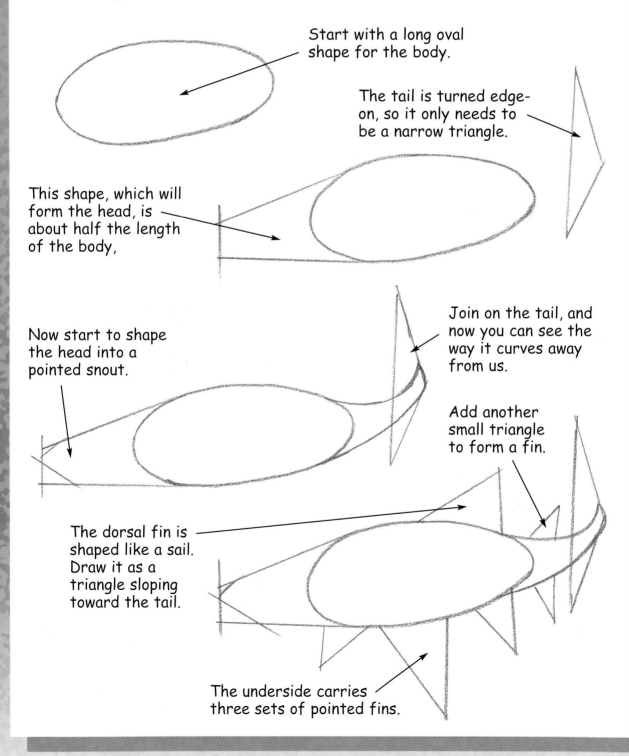

Start with a long oval shape for the body.

The tail is turned edge-on, so it only needs to be a narrow triangle.

This shape, which will form the head, is about half the length of the body,

Now start to shape the head into a pointed snout.

Join on the tail, and now you can see the way it curves away from us.

Add another small triangle to form a fin.

The dorsal fin is shaped like a sail. Draw it as a triangle sloping toward the tail.

The underside carries three sets of pointed fins.

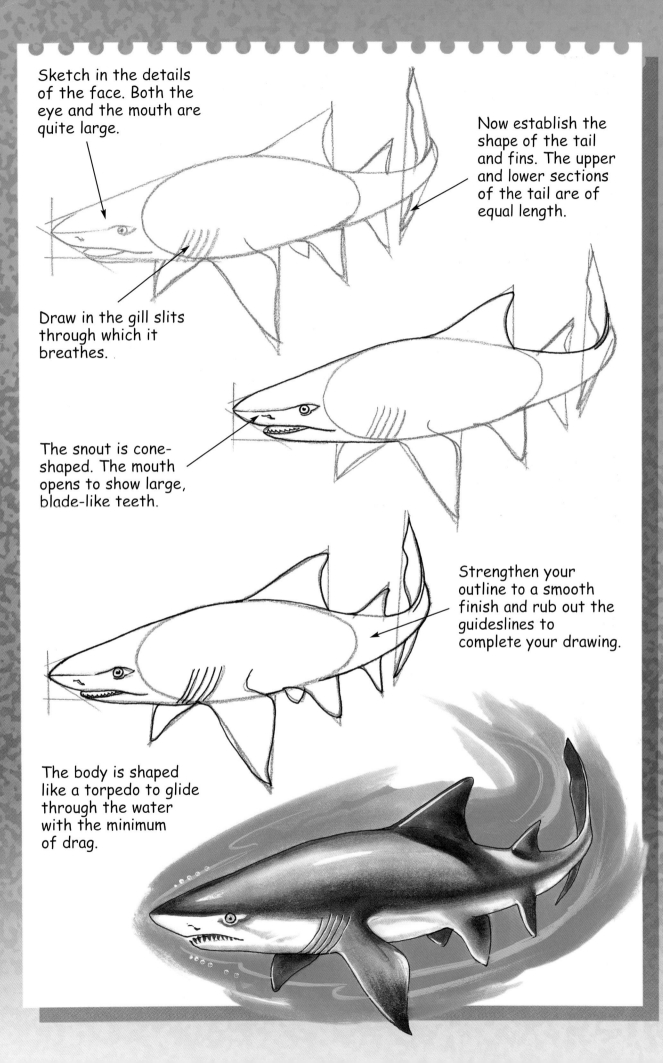

Sketch in the details of the face. Both the eye and the mouth are quite large.

Now establish the shape of the tail and fins. The upper and lower sections of the tail are of equal length.

Draw in the gill slits through which it breathes.

The snout is cone-shaped. The mouth opens to show large, blade-like teeth.

Strengthen your outline to a smooth finish and rub out the guideslines to complete your drawing.

The body is shaped like a torpedo to glide through the water with the minimum of drag.

Hammerhead Shark

You only have to look at a Hammerhead to see how it got its name. The strange, flattened head extends on either side to form a shape just like a hammer.

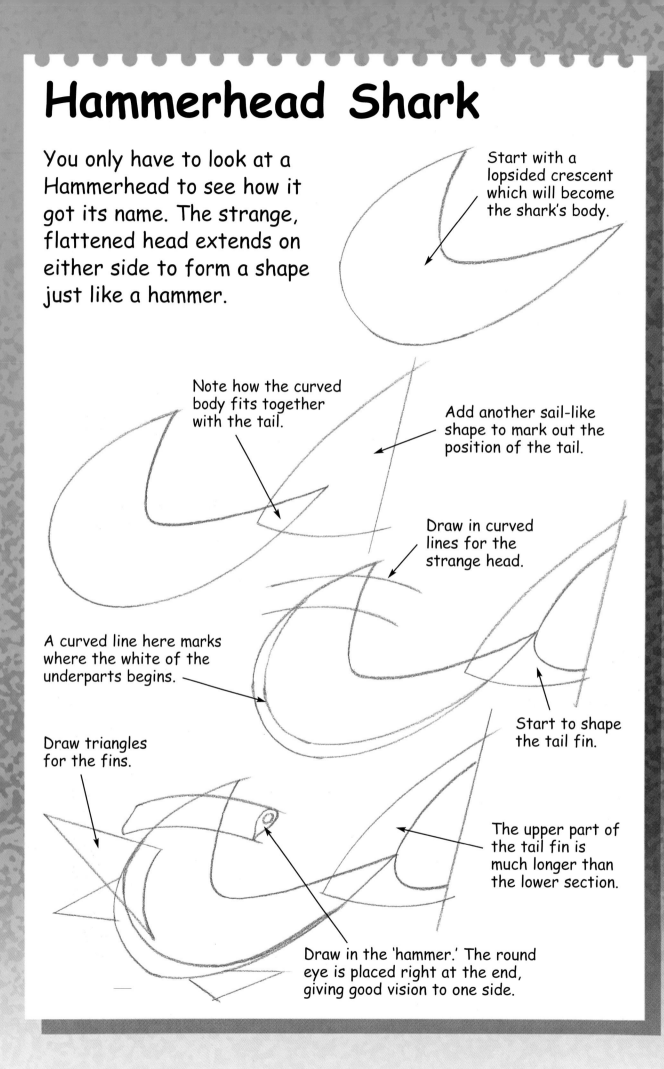

Start with a lopsided crescent which will become the shark's body.

Note how the curved body fits together with the tail.

Add another sail-like shape to mark out the position of the tail.

Draw in curved lines for the strange head.

A curved line here marks where the white of the underparts begins.

Start to shape the tail fin.

Draw triangles for the fins.

The upper part of the tail fin is much longer than the lower section.

Draw in the 'hammer.' The round eye is placed right at the end, giving good vision to one side.

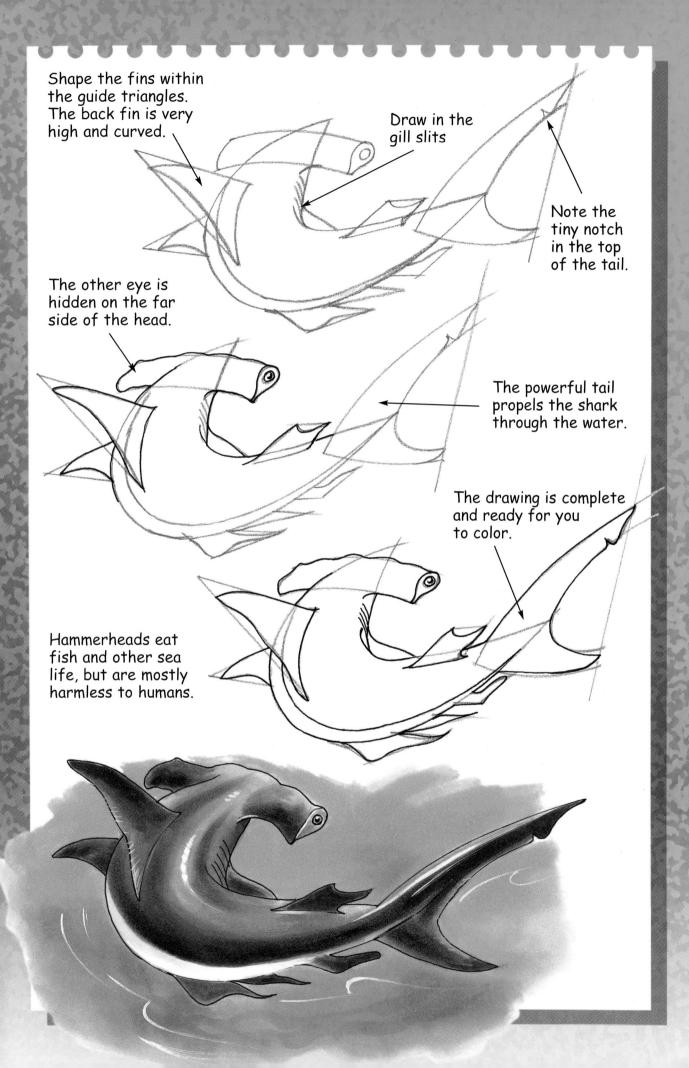

Shape the fins within the guide triangles. The back fin is very high and curved.

Draw in the gill slits

Note the tiny notch in the top of the tail.

The other eye is hidden on the far side of the head.

The powerful tail propels the shark through the water.

The drawing is complete and ready for you to color.

Hammerheads eat fish and other sea life, but are mostly harmless to humans.

Great White Shark

This is the biggest and most dangerous of all sharks. It hunts large prey like seals and dolphins – and sometimes attacks humans. Most people know this shark best as the giant man-eater in the film *Jaws*.

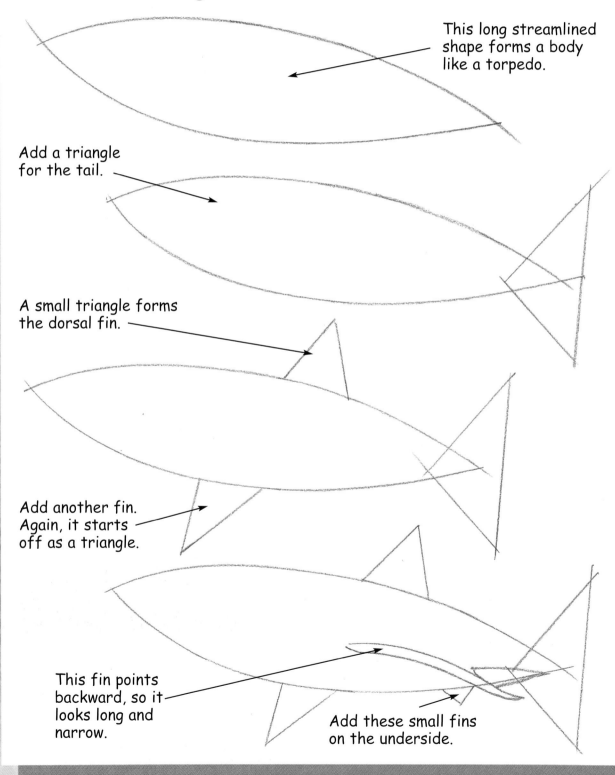

This long streamlined shape forms a body like a torpedo.

Add a triangle for the tail.

A small triangle forms the dorsal fin.

Add another fin. Again, it starts off as a triangle.

This fin points backward, so it looks long and narrow.

Add these small fins on the underside.

The snout is shaped like a blunt cone.

Mark out the line between the gray back and the white underparts.

Draw in the curved mouth.

The eye is small but the Great White has excellent vision.

Start to shape the tail fin.

Make your outline strong and smooth and finish off all the detail. Don't forget those razor-sharp teeth.

The strong tail provides driving force to propel the shark through the water swiftly.

Also known as 'White Death,' the Great White shark is feared more than any of the 370 species of shark living today.

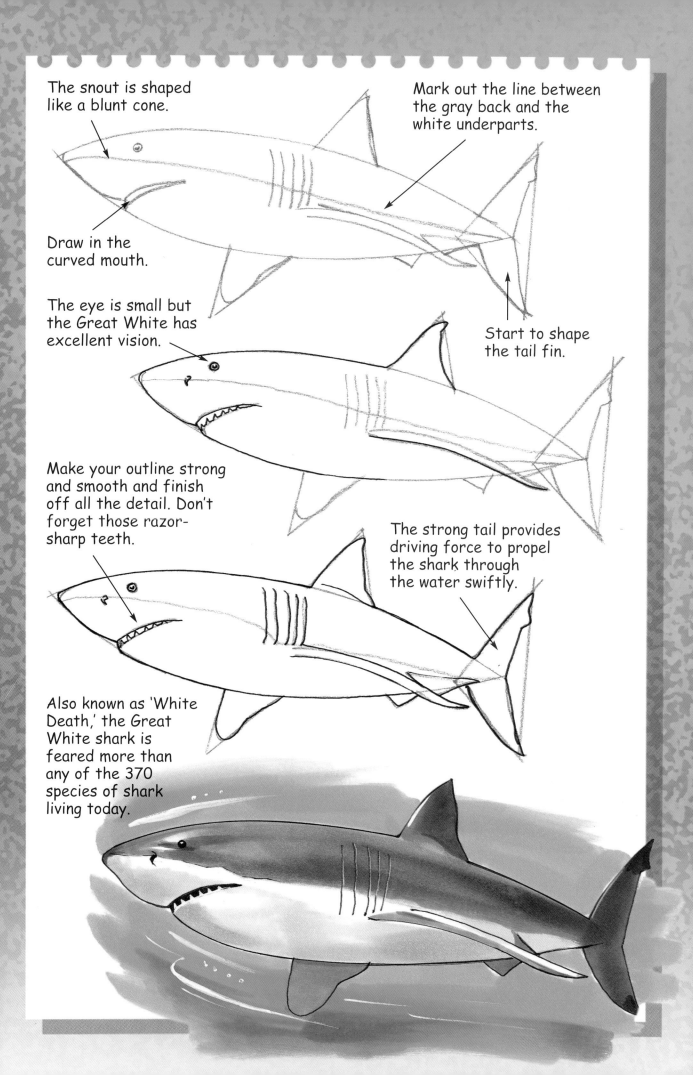

Humpback Whale

Humpback Whales are famous for their 'songs.' They 'talk' to each other underwater in musical-sounding clicks. Despite its large size, the Humpback feeds only on tiny sea creatures. A built-in sieve at the back of its mouth allows it to filter these out from mouthfuls of sea water.

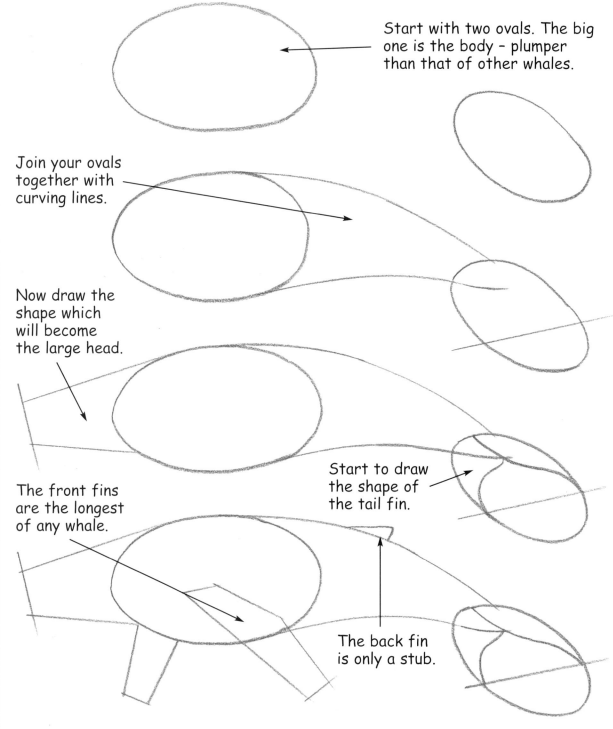

Start with two ovals. The big one is the body – plumper than that of other whales.

Join your ovals together with curving lines.

Now draw the shape which will become the large head.

Start to draw the shape of the tail fin.

The front fins are the longest of any whale.

The back fin is only a stub.

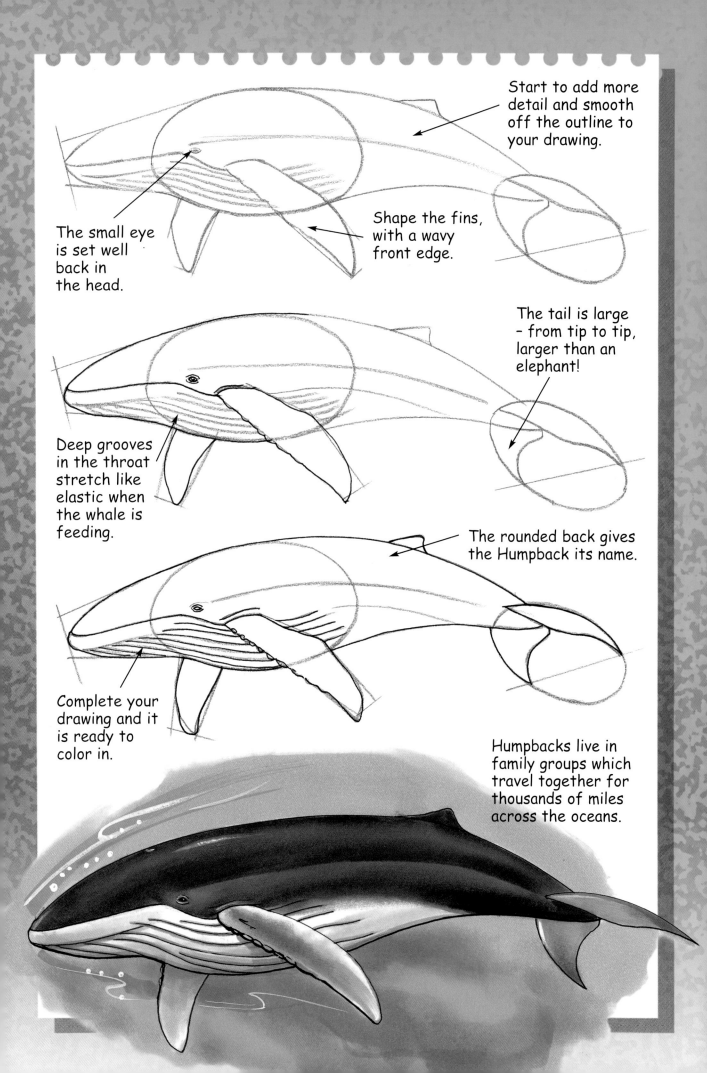

Start to add more detail and smooth off the outline to your drawing.

The small eye is set well back in the head.

Shape the fins, with a wavy front edge.

The tail is large – from tip to tip, larger than an elephant!

Deep grooves in the throat stretch like elastic when the whale is feeding.

The rounded back gives the Humpback its name.

Complete your drawing and it is ready to color in.

Humpbacks live in family groups which travel together for thousands of miles across the oceans.

Fin Whale

This is the second-largest living whale. But, like the Humpback, the Fin Whale feeds on tiny sea creatures which it sieves out of the water. It also hunts small fish, like herrings, which it herds together like a sheepdog before gulping them down.

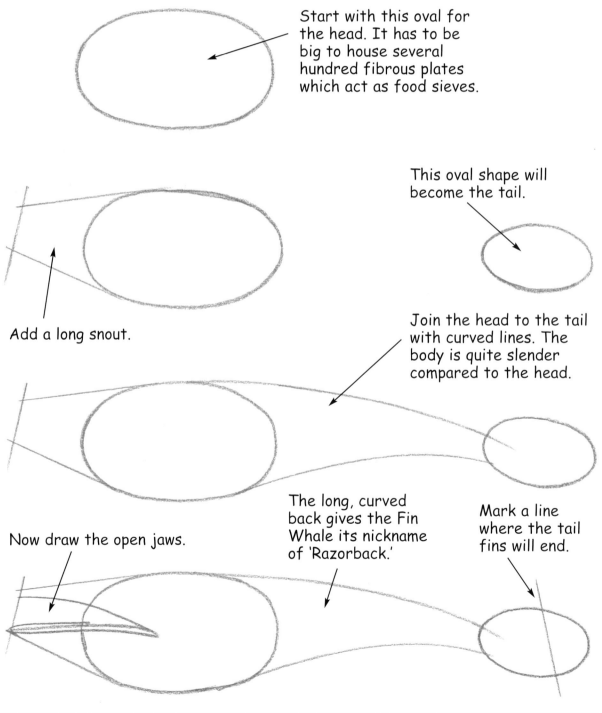

Start with this oval for the head. It has to be big to house several hundred fibrous plates which act as food sieves.

This oval shape will become the tail.

Add a long snout.

Join the head to the tail with curved lines. The body is quite slender compared to the head.

Now draw the open jaws.

The long, curved back gives the Fin Whale its nickname of 'Razorback.'

Mark a line where the tail fins will end.

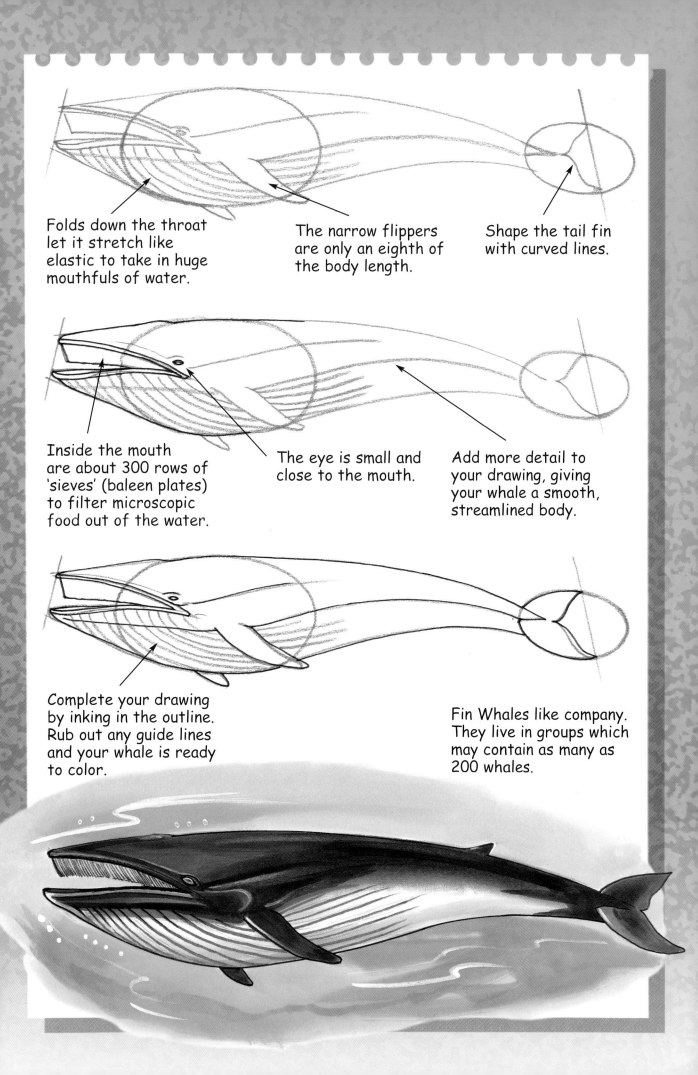

Folds down the throat let it stretch like elastic to take in huge mouthfuls of water.

The narrow flippers are only an eighth of the body length.

Shape the tail fin with curved lines.

Inside the mouth are about 300 rows of 'sieves' (baleen plates) to filter microscopic food out of the water.

The eye is small and close to the mouth.

Add more detail to your drawing, giving your whale a smooth, streamlined body.

Complete your drawing by inking in the outline. Rub out any guide lines and your whale is ready to color.

Fin Whales like company. They live in groups which may contain as many as 200 whales.

Killer Whale

The black and white Killer Whale is not actually a whale at all, but a member of the dolphin family. Large groups of Killers hunt in fierce packs to attack seals, porpoises, and even whales. But tame Killers have shown themselves to be as intelligent and friendly as more popular dolphins.

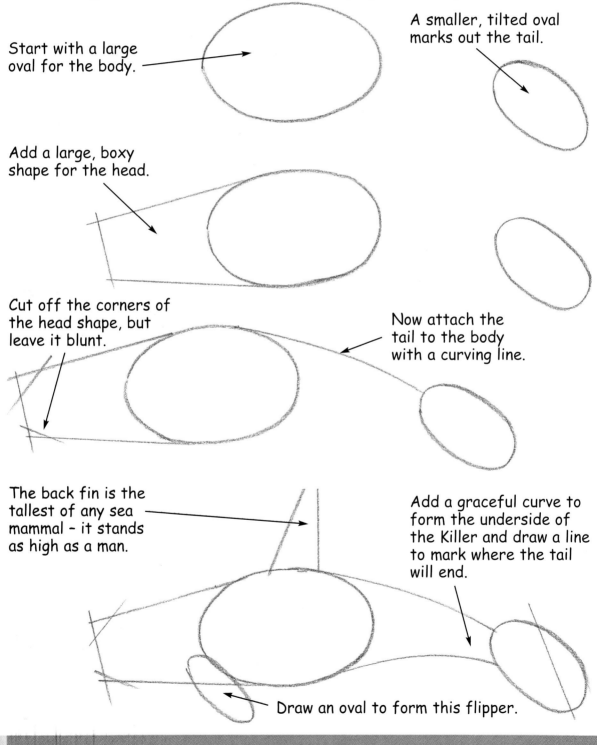

Start with a large oval for the body.

A smaller, tilted oval marks out the tail.

Add a large, boxy shape for the head.

Cut off the corners of the head shape, but leave it blunt.

Now attach the tail to the body with a curving line.

The back fin is the tallest of any sea mammal – it stands as high as a man.

Add a graceful curve to form the underside of the Killer and draw a line to mark where the tail will end.

Draw an oval to form this flipper.

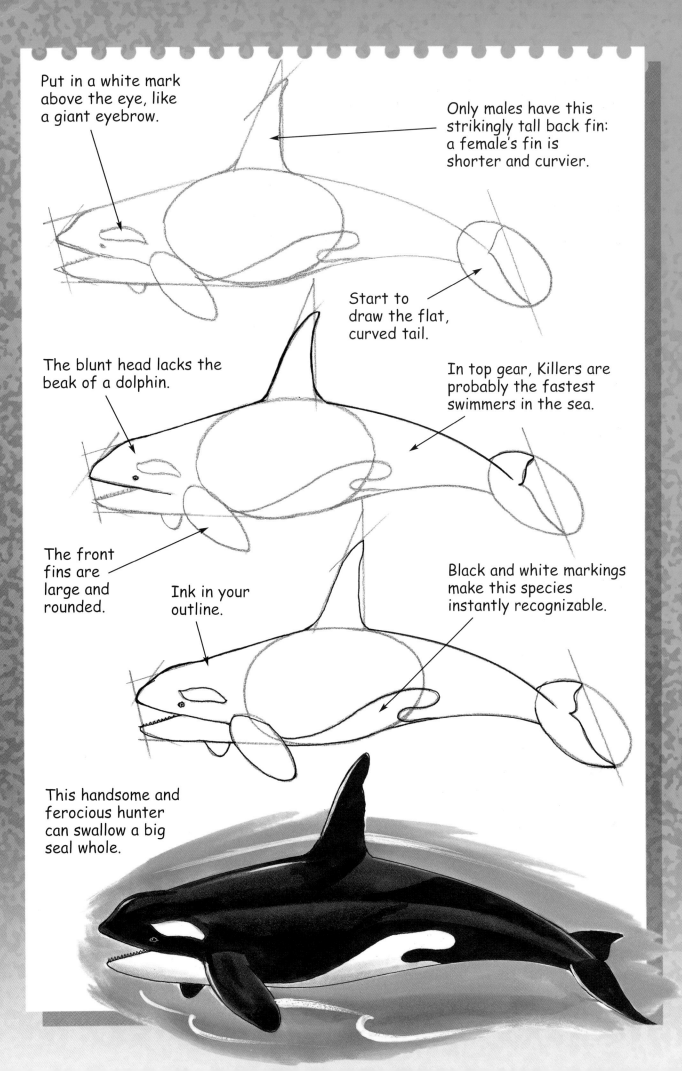

Put in a white mark above the eye, like a giant eyebrow.

Only males have this strikingly tall back fin: a female's fin is shorter and curvier.

Start to draw the flat, curved tail.

The blunt head lacks the beak of a dolphin.

In top gear, Killers are probably the fastest swimmers in the sea.

The front fins are large and rounded.

Ink in your outline.

Black and white markings make this species instantly recognizable.

This handsome and ferocious hunter can swallow a big seal whole.

Blue Shark

Blue Sharks like deep water. They keep far out to sea, so bathers near the beach are safe. But, although their main diet is fish, they will eat anything – turtles, crabs, garbage, or humans. So divers in deep waters, and shipwreck victims, are at risk from Blue Shark attacks.

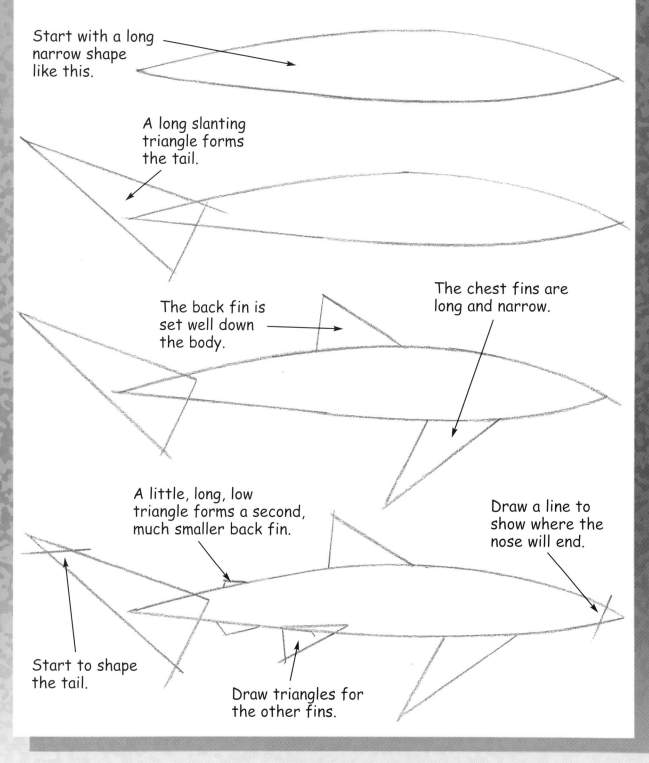

Start with a long narrow shape like this.

A long slanting triangle forms the tail.

The back fin is set well down the body.

The chest fins are long and narrow.

A little, long, low triangle forms a second, much smaller back fin.

Draw a line to show where the nose will end.

Start to shape the tail.

Draw triangles for the other fins.

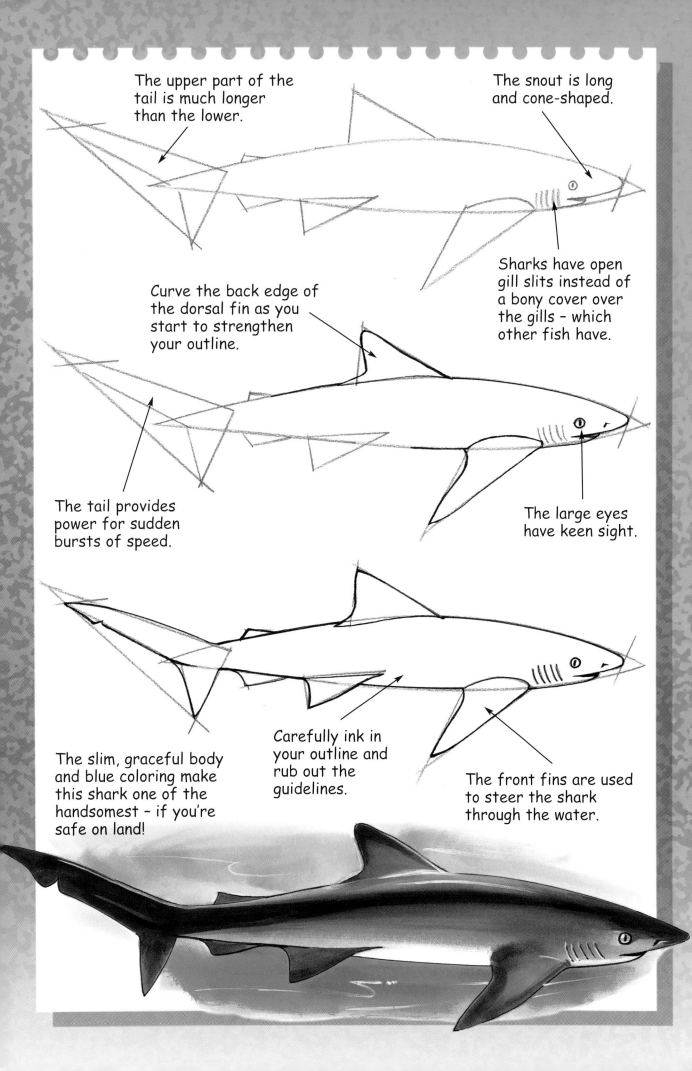

The upper part of the tail is much longer than the lower.

The snout is long and cone-shaped.

Sharks have open gill slits instead of a bony cover over the gills – which other fish have.

Curve the back edge of the dorsal fin as you start to strengthen your outline.

The tail provides power for sudden bursts of speed.

The large eyes have keen sight.

The slim, graceful body and blue coloring make this shark one of the handsomest – if you're safe on land!

Carefully ink in your outline and rub out the guidelines.

The front fins are used to steer the shark through the water.

River Dolphin

River Dolphins live in the rivers of Asia and South America. Unable to hunt by sight in these muddy waters, they have developed radar, like bats. They 'see' underwater objects by aiming high-pitched clicking sounds at them and detecting the echoes as they bounce back.

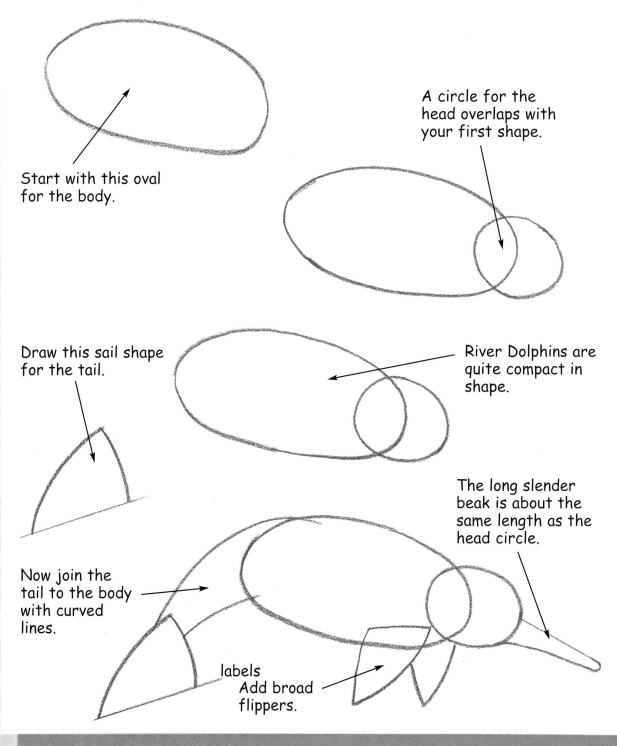

Start with this oval for the body.

A circle for the head overlaps with your first shape.

Draw this sail shape for the tail.

River Dolphins are quite compact in shape.

The long slender beak is about the same length as the head circle.

Now join the tail to the body with curved lines.

labels
Add broad flippers.

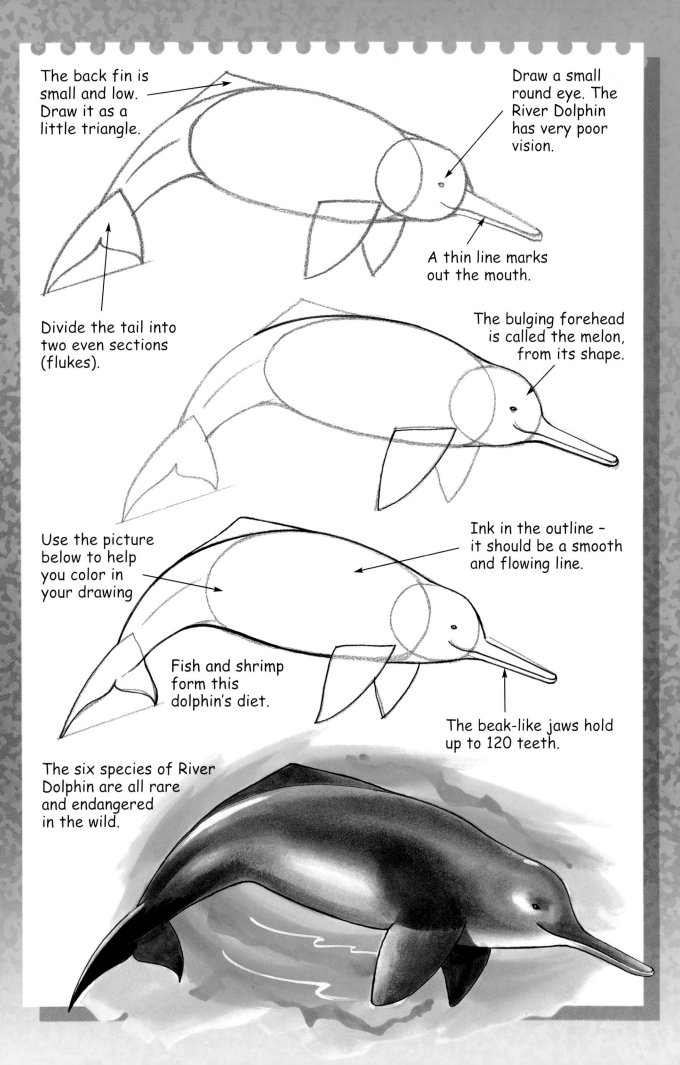

The back fin is small and low. Draw it as a little triangle.

Draw a small round eye. The River Dolphin has very poor vision.

A thin line marks out the mouth.

Divide the tail into two even sections (flukes).

The bulging forehead is called the melon, from its shape.

Use the picture below to help you color in your drawing

Ink in the outline – it should be a smooth and flowing line.

Fish and shrimp form this dolphin's diet.

The beak-like jaws hold up to 120 teeth.

The six species of River Dolphin are all rare and endangered in the wild.

Gray Reef Shark

This shark belongs to the same family as the Blue and Tiger Sharks. Like them, it is a fierce hunter which attacks a wide range of prey. It takes its name from the coral reefs where it usually lives, hunting reef fish, octopus, and crabs.

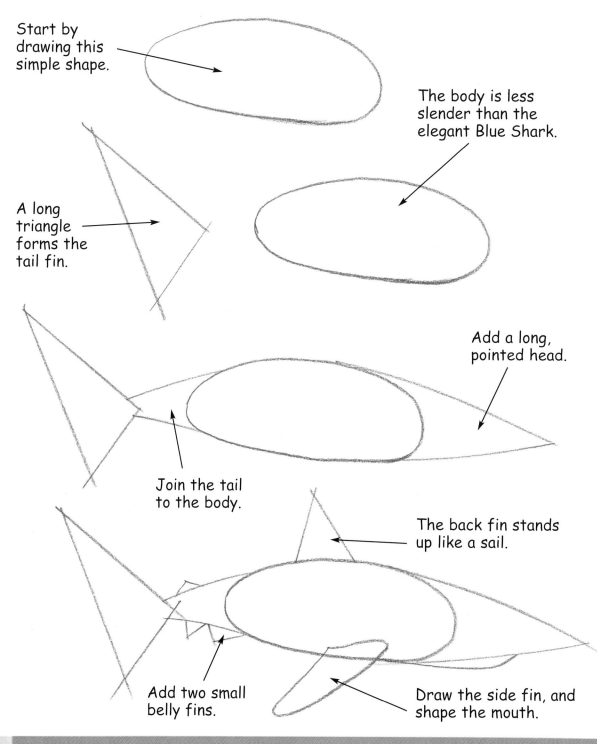

Start by drawing this simple shape.

The body is less slender than the elegant Blue Shark.

A long triangle forms the tail fin.

Add a long, pointed head.

Join the tail to the body.

The back fin stands up like a sail.

Add two small belly fins.

Draw the side fin, and shape the mouth.

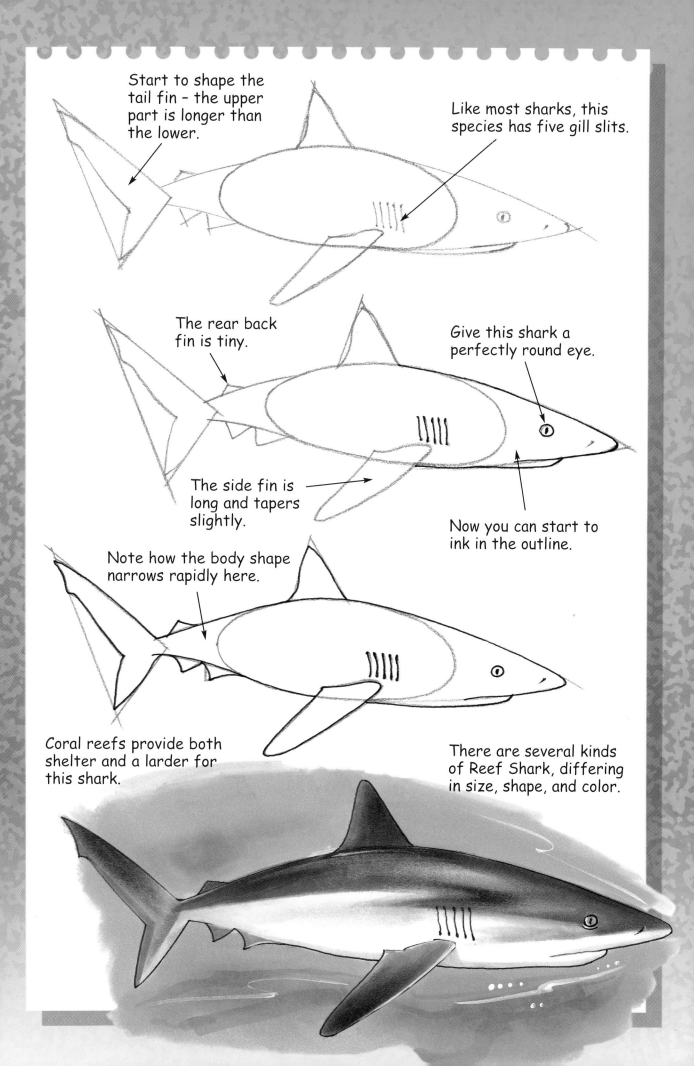

Start to shape the tail fin – the upper part is longer than the lower.

Like most sharks, this species has five gill slits.

The rear back fin is tiny.

Give this shark a perfectly round eye.

The side fin is long and tapers slightly.

Now you can start to ink in the outline.

Note how the body shape narrows rapidly here.

Coral reefs provide both shelter and a larder for this shark.

There are several kinds of Reef Shark, differing in size, shape, and color.

Bottlenose Whale

There are many kinds of Beaked Whales, with long, beak-like snouts. As its name suggests, the Bottlenose has the most oddly shaped beak of all. Its whole head is unusual, with a huge bulging forehead which makes the long beak beneath it look just like the neck of a bottle.

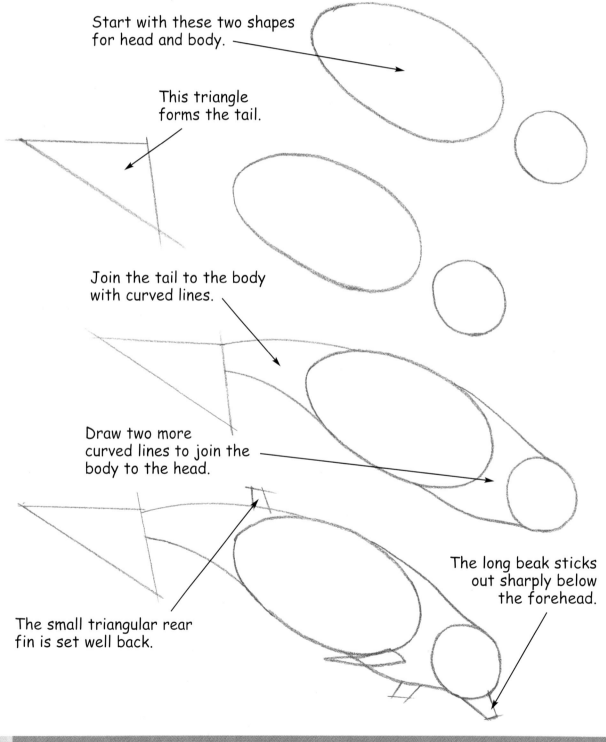

Start with these two shapes for head and body.

This triangle forms the tail.

Join the tail to the body with curved lines.

Draw two more curved lines to join the body to the head.

The long beak sticks out sharply below the forehead.

The small triangular rear fin is set well back.

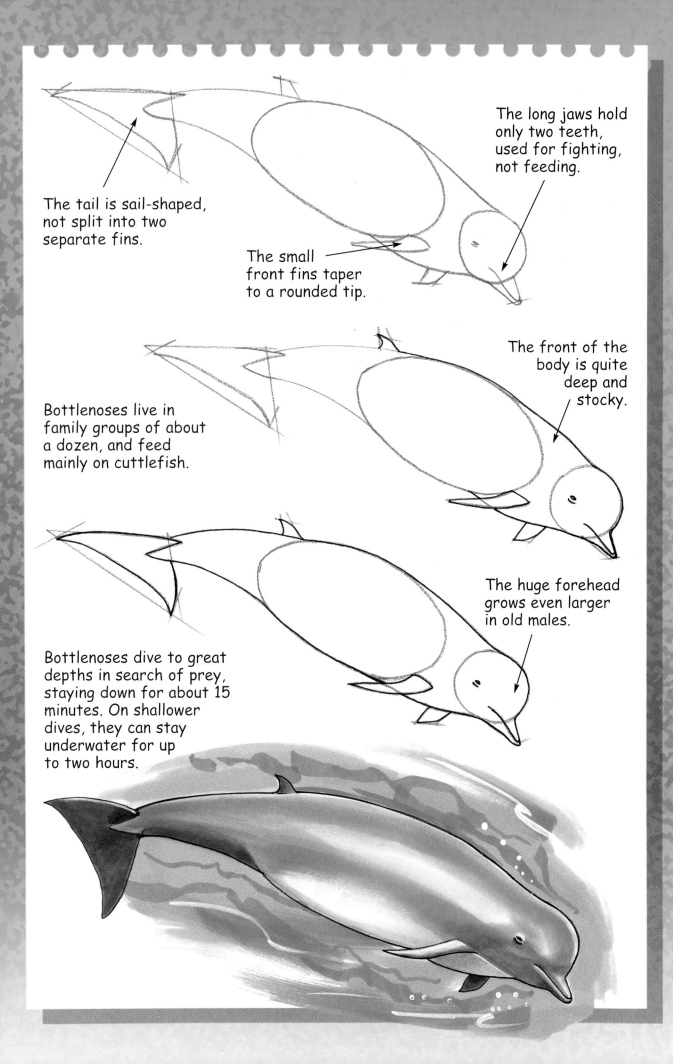

The long jaws hold only two teeth, used for fighting, not feeding.

The tail is sail-shaped, not split into two separate fins.

The small front fins taper to a rounded tip.

Bottlenoses live in family groups of about a dozen, and feed mainly on cuttlefish.

The front of the body is quite deep and stocky.

The huge forehead grows even larger in old males.

Bottlenoses dive to great depths in search of prey, staying down for about 15 minutes. On shallower dives, they can stay underwater for up to two hours.